Storms and Silence

Kayla Krambeck

BookLeaf
Publishing

Presentation by *BookLeaf Publishing*

Web: www.bookleafpub.com

E-mail: info@bookleafpub.com

ISBN: 9789357744829

First edition 2023

To life and love.

ACKNOWLEDGEMENT

To those who have supported me in my journey.
To Mark for helping me with a title.

Fractured

Sitting on the floor.
A sea of blank squares.
Everything is white.
Blank. Empty.
There is no color here.

Pieces lie scattered.
A mirror. Fractured.
They call to me.
Whisper strongly.
I reach out for them.

Look into their faces.
Reflections bounce back.
Myself. My life.
My ghosts. My dreams.
I must mend the cracks.

Where to begin?
Pick up a shard.
It is heavy. Weighted.
Sharp pain explodes.
My hands bleed.

Not my hands. My heart.

Pierced by the shard.
A gaping hole.
I drop the shard-
Then pick up another.

Piece after piece
Each one cuts, bleeds.
My head is swimming.
I feel trapped.
I search-No escape.

Splattered in red.
I see them.
Fractured shards of me.
Of my heart, my mind.
Unable to mend.

Unable to hold them.
I watch the pieces bleed.
Feel the pain. Anger.
Grief. Fear.
Fractures of me.

Color of Grief

The color of grief
Is blue
Like the storm-tossed
Sea.

Like the bright blue
Flames
That devour things
Lost.

The color of grief
Is grey
Like the wind-driven
Clouds.

Like the thick grey
Fog
That blocks out
Light.

The color of grief
Is black
Like an endless
Night.

Like the still, empty
Void
That eats up
Hope.

To Fly

Ah, to fly!
With wings unfurled

Like eagles soaring
With feathers of flight

Like butterflies fluttering
With steady might

Like dragons gliding
With scales of light

If only I
Could be so free

Ah, to fly!

Sounds of Life

I sit in silence and
Listen to its sound

I hear the breeze
Dance gently through leaves

I hear feathered wings
Flutter swiftly above

I hear the river
Bubble over the rocks

I hear the buzz
Of the bumblebee's flight

I hear my heart
Beating strong like a drum

Jewels of the Earth

As the sun rises
Above the horizon
I glance at my feet

Reaching far beyond
My own human sight
Are millions of jewels

Necklaces of deep pink and red
Rings of pure blue and white
Bracelets of lush emerald

Resting atop these pristine petals
Sit millions of diamonds
Glittering in the day's new light

Dewdrops of life
Kiss the petals awake
In a glaze of love

No gold nor silver
Or gemstones galore
Could ever compare
To jewels on the earth's floor

Memories

Memories are unpredictable
Gathering here and there
Collecting webs of scars
Like old forgotten books

Their covers are blank
Leaving you wondering
If the journey will be
Pleasant or painful

You open the cover
And turn the first page
Where you find yourself
Thrust into a maze of woe

Crashing and stumbling
Gasping for breath
Until the final page
Reads "the end"

There are covers of collage
Behind whose pages are skewered
Into fragments of images
With no sense of time

A sea of drifting pieces
Tossing you from left to right
While you frantically reach
Out hoping for a life raft

Others are more gentle
Delicately guiding you down
A path of joy and laughter
That leaves you breathless

Strolling down a lane
Until you reach the end
Wishing for more love
And yearning for more life

Life of Shadows

Life of Shadows
Dawn once so bright now strewn with pain
Dwindling hope now surrenders to despair

Morning brings storms with clouds of ebony and
grey
Torrents of rain carry drops of negative energy

Molded as from lightning, thoughts strike the
mind
Deafening roars of hate thunder through the soul

Heart open and feeling, now embedded in stone
Fortress of cold steel holds captive the light

Life no longer precious balances on the edge
Hanging thin on thread pleading for rescue

Wracked with endless strife, fraught with
confusion deep
Paths once known within dispelled by
everlasting grief

An ending now sought, brings forth new chaos

Promise of sweet release now beckons the
forlorn

Arms now wide open, death probes the heart
Offering of desired peace, unyielding in pure
rest

Twisted Worlds

First created by light, transformed into dark
Time spent in shadow ere long now breaks

Light held captive breaks forth in waves
Florescent with power strong shining boldly
through dark

Worlds engaged as forces struggle to gain
victory
Heart once chained pushes towards light now
unbending

Darkness swirls broad amongst condensed
beams of light
Beauty and beast now enemies collide in a battle

Heart covered in stone soon stained with blood
Soul lost and confused overrun with emotion
ripe

Through time passing on light rallies forth
renewed
Though battle cries ring hope softens the blow

Despite newborn hope darkness battles on
within
Demons in number rush forward with swords
sharp

Swim rivers deep in sorrow built upon pain
Traverse mountain tops capped in white peace

Heart once so numb now beats with life
Two worlds now twisted in the soul

Creature of Dark

Born into the light your meaning was love
A world of laughter soon lost in shadow

As darkness grew slow so light quickly faded
Until light at long last once alive now lost

Deep within the abyss of despair where
Dark now abounds light flees far

Deeper trenches of pain fill sleepless nights
Abounding in a darkness empty of hope

Swirling with grief in claws of confusion
Thirsty for relief unfound chained to the past

The cage once loathed becomes a new home
Light won over by shadows so dark

Emergence

Veins pulse with fear as feet step forward
Tentative hands reach out in the chosen path

Hope of life-filled freedom floats on air
Hands tremble in fear as memories rise forth

Strength renewed by love's healing touch
Wings bent and chained released link by link

Once held captive now freed from cold steel
Cries rush forth while engulfed in blazing fire

Brilliant flames lick the wounds once so deep
Scarred creature reduced to smoldering ash

Radiance

From smoldering ashes she rises in radiance
Eyes glowing bright, wings spread open wide

Body and soul on fire alighting to the sky
Free from fear, pain, and despair

Eyes filled with untamed freedom and joy
Smile dancing with laughter and singing

Voice ringing with confidence and love
Mind powered in sweet clarity and peace

Soaring high on wings laced with fire
Veins of gold mark the scars of the past

Body brimming in unharnessed boldness
Fire and water mesh within her soul

Bound no more by chains she flies eagerly
Reborn anew as a radiant creature

Song of Trees

If I listen closely
To the voice of
The trees

I can hear their
Song ringing softly
In the breeze

They sing of
Rain and drought
And frigid freeze

They sing of
Life growing
In new leaves

Their song tells
Tales of battles
Won with ease

Their song gives
Hope to those
On fallen knees

Rage

I feel it sitting inside
Like a caged tiger sleeping
With one eye open

Always watching for an open door
To slither out and wreak havoc
On an unsuspecting victim

Its strength is full
From the wound of
Childhood pain

Full of the ache of
Abandonment and
The grief of loneliness

I cannot let it loose
To destroy the good
And devour the love

But I cannot
Let it grow inside
Where it rots the heart

So where do I place

This insidious beast
That seeks to destroy?

Touch of Love

The touch of love is
Filled with joy that lights the eyes

It shines a lamp on
Darkened alleys of the mind

It brings forth hope in
The dampened heart

It gently caresses the
Sun-soaked skin

It whispers softly
To the lonely kind

It wholly heals the
Weary worn soul

Earth

21

Rich hues of brown, black
Red, gold, and white

Soft as velvet against the skin
Warm as sunlight in the air

Casting out its fragrant scent
As I cradle a scoopful in my hands

Canyon of Depression

Some canyons tunnel so deep
The light no longer touches the life

You peer upwards or at least
In the direction you think is up

Only to find looming walls
Growing endless towards the sky

There is no light on the floor
Of the canyon so deep

But you keep walking in search
Of an end, an exit, a staircase

A way out of the dark
Far from its hopeless tendrils

Away from its piercing claws
Of death and despair

When the storms come in the
Canyon floods sweep you astray

Drowning you wave after wave

Until you are gasping for air

Over and over the canyon fills
Day after day, year after year

Until you no longer recognize
Your reflection in the mirror

Playful Peace

High-pitched squeals and giggles
Ring out amidst bursts of wind

Joyfully breathing in and out
As though my lungs have just awoken

I chase the butterflies in their gowns
As they dance from flower to flower

I lift my head to the rain as it
Washes away the strain of the world

I race sticks in the current of
Rivers sailing gracefully by

I sit happily under the arms of
The great oak trees breathing in peace

Courage

Courage is not always a
Brazen war cry yelled out

Courage is stepping forward
On the path of healing

Courage is choosing to
Rise out of bed each day

Courage is deciding to be
Kind in the face of pain

Courage is walking towards an
Uncertain future only imagined

Courage is smiling through
The clouds of life and love

Courage is promising yourself
You will never yield to the trauma

Courage is a quiet whisper
Reminding you there is always tomorrow

Sound of Silence

www.ingramcontent.com/pod-product-compliance
Lightning Source LLC
LaVergne TN
LVHW021343200726
843509LV00014B/2644